Sketch of the Mythology of the North American Indians

by

John Wesley

THE GENESIS OF PHILOSOPHY.

The wonders of the course of nature have ever challenged attention. In savagery, in barbarism, and in civilization alike, the mind of man has sought the explanation of things. The movements of the heavenly bodies, the change of seasons, the succession of night and day, the powers of the air, majestic mountains, ever-flowing rivers, perennial springs, the flight of birds, the gliding of serpents, the growth of trees, the blooming of flowers, the forms of storm-carved rocks, the mysteries of life and death, the institutions of society—many are the things to be explained. The yearning to know is universal. *How* and *why* are everlasting interrogatories profoundly instinct in humanity. In the evolution of the human mind, the instinct of cosmic interrogation follows hard upon the instinct of self-preservation.

In all the operations of nature, man's weal and woe are involved. A cold wave sweeps from the north—rivers and lakes are frozen, forests are buried under snows, and the fierce winds almost congeal the life-fluids of man himself, and indeed man's sources of supply are buried under the rocks of water. At another time the heavens are as brass, and the clouds come and go with mockery of unfulfilled promises of rain, the fierce midsummer sun pours its beams upon the sands, and blasts heated in the furnace of the desert sear the vegetation; and the fruits, which in more congenial seasons are subsistence and luxury, shrivel before the eyes of famishing men. A river rages and destroys the adjacent valley with its flood. A mountain bursts forth with its rivers of fire, the land is buried and the people are swept away. Lightning shivers a tree and rends a skull. The silent, unseen powers of nature, too, are at work bringing pain or joy, health or sickness, life or death, to mankind. In like manner man's welfare is involved in all the institutions of society. *How* and *why* are the questions asked about all these things—questions [Pg 20]springing from the deepest instinct of self-preservation.

In all stages of savage, barbaric, and civilized inquiry, every question has found an answer, every *how* has had its *thus*, every *why* its *because*. The sum of the answers to the questions raised by any people constitute its philosophy; hence all peoples have had philosophies consisting of their accepted explanation of things. Such a philosophy must necessarily result from the primary instincts developed in man in the early progress of his differentiation from the beast. This I postulate: if demonstration is necessary, demonstration is at hand. Not only has every people a philosophy, but every stage of culture is characterized by its stage of philosophy. Philosophy has been unfolded with the evolution of the human understanding. The history of philosophy is the history of human opinions from the earlier to the later days—from the lower to the higher culture.

In the production of a philosophy, phenomena must be *discerned, discriminated, classified*. Discernment, discrimination, and classification are the processes by which a philosophy is developed. In studying the philosophy of a people at any stage of culture, to understand what such a people entertain as the sum of their knowledge, it is necessary that we should understand what phenomena they saw, heard, felt, discerned; what discriminations they made, and what resemblances they seized upon as a basis for the classification on which their explanations rested. A philosophy will be higher in the scale, nearer the truth, as the discernment is wider, the discrimination nicer, and the classification better.

The sense of the savage is dull compared with the sense of the civilized man. There is a myth current in civilization to the effect that the barbarian has highly developed perceptive faculties. It has no more foundation than the myth of the wisdom of the owl. A savage sees but few sights, hears but few sounds, tastes but few flavors, smells but few odors; his whole sensuous life is narrow and blunt, and his facts that are made up of the combination of sensuous impressions are few. In comparison, the civilized man has his vision extended away toward the infinitesimal and away toward the infinite; his perception of sound is multiplied to the comprehension of rapturous symphonies; his perception of taste is increased to the enjoyment of delicious viands; his perception of smell is developed to the appreciation of most exquisite perfumes; and his facts that are made up of the combination of sensuous impressions are multiplied beyond enumeration. The stages of discernment from the lowest savage to the highest civilized man constitute a series the end of which is far from the beginning.

If the discernment of the savage is little, his discrimination is less. All his sensuous perceptions are confused; but the confusion of confusion is that universal habit of savagery—the confusion of the objective with the subjective—so that the savage sees, hears, tastes, smells, feels the imaginings of his own mind. Subjectively determined sensuous processes are diseases in civilization, but normal, functional [Pg 21]methods in savagery.

The savage philosopher classifies by obvious resemblances—analogic characters. The civilized philosopher classifies by essential affinitives—homologic characteristics—and the progress of philosophy is marked by changes from analogic categories to homologic categories.

TWO GRAND STAGES OF PHILOSOPHY.

There are two grand stages of philosophy—the mythologic and scientific. In the first, all phenomena are explained by analogies derived from subjective human experiences; in the latter, phenomena are explained as orderly successions of events.

In sublime egotism, man first interprets the cosmos as an extension of himself; he classifies the phenomena of the outer word by their analogies with subjective phenomena; his measure of distance is his own pace, his measure of time his own sleep, for he says, "It is a thousand paces to the great rock," or, "It is a hundred sleeps to the great feast." Noises are voices, powers are hands, movements are made afoot. By subjective examination discovering in himself will and design, and by inductive reason discovering will and design in his fellow men and in animals, he extends the induction to all the cosmos, and there discovers in all things will and design. All phenomena are supposed to be the acts of some one, and that some one having will and purpose. In mythologic philosophy the phenomena of the outer physical world are supposed to be the acts of living, willing, designing personages. The simple are compared with and explained by the complex. In scientific philosophy, phenomena are supposed to be children of antecedent phenomena, and so far as science goes with its explanation they are thus interpreted. Man with the subjective phenomena gathered about him is studied from an objective point of view, and the phenomena of subjective life are relegated to the categories established in the classification of the phenomena of the outer world; thus the complex is studied by resolving it into its simple constituents.

There is an unknown known, and there is a known unknown. The unknown known is the philosophy of savagery; the known unknown is the philosophy of civilization. In those stages of culture that we call savagery and barbarism, all things are known—supposed to be known; but when at last something is known, understood, explained, then to those who have that knowledge in full comprehension all other things become unknown. Then is ushered in the era of investigation and discovery; then science is born; then is the beginning of civilization. The philosophy of savagery is complete; the philosophy of civilization fragmentary. Ye men of science, [Pg 22]ye wise fools, ye have discovered the law of gravity, but ye cannot tell what gravity is. But savagery has a cause and a method for all things; nothing is left unexplained.

In the lower stages of savagery the cosmos is bounded by the great plain of land and sea on which we tread, and the firmament, the azure surface above, set with brilliants; and beyond is an abyss of—nothing. Within these bounds all things are known, all things are explained; there are no mysteries but the whims of the gods. But when the plain on which we tread becomes a portion of the surface of a great globe, and the domed firmament becomes the heavens, stretching beyond Alcyone and Sirius, with this enlargement of the realm of philosophy the verity of philosophy is questioned. The savage is a positive man; the scientist is a doubting man.

The opinions of a savage people are childish. Society grows! Some say society develops; others that society evolves; but, somehow, I like to say it grows. The history of the discovery of growth is a large part of the history of human culture. That individuals grow, that the child grows to be a man, the colt a horse, the scion a tree, is easily recognized, though with unassisted eye the processes of growth are not discovered. But that races grow—races of men, races of animals, races of plants, races or groups of worlds—is a very late discovery, and yet all of us do not grasp so great a thought. Consider that stage of culture where the growth of individuals is not fully recognized. That stage is savagery. To-day the native races of North America are agitated by discussions over that great philosophic question, "Do the trees grow or were they created?" That the grass grows they admit, but the orthodox philosophers stoutly assert that the forest pines and the great *sequoias* were created as they are.

Thus in savagery the philosophers dispute over the immediate creation or development of individuals—in civilization over the immediate creation or development of races. I know of no single fact that better illustrates the wide difference between these two stages of culture. But let us look for other terms of comparison. The scalping scene is no more the true picture of savagery than the bayonet charge of civilization. Savagery is sylvan life. Contrast *Ka-ni-ga* with New York. *Ka-ni-ga* is an Indian village in the Rocky Mountains. New York is, well—New York. The home in the forest is a shelter of boughs; the home in New York is a palace of granite. The dwellers in *Ka-ni-ga* are clothed in the skins of animals, rudely tanned, rudely wrought, and colored with daubs of clay. For the garments of New York, flocks are tended, fields are cultivated, ships sail on the sea, and men dig in the mountains for dye-stuffs stored in the rocks. The industries of *Ka-ni-ga* employ stone knives, bone awls, and human muscle; the industries of New York employ the tools of the trades, the machinery of the manufactories, and the power of the sun—for water-power is but sunshine, and the coal mine [Pg 23]is but a pot of pickeled sunbeams.

Even the nursery rhymes are in contrast; the prattler in New York says:

Daffy down dilly
Has come up to town,
With a green petticoat
And a blue gown;

but in savagery the outer and nether garments are not yet differentiated; and more: blue and green are not differentiated, for the Indian has but one name for the two; the green grass and the blue heavens are of the same hue in the Indian tongue. But the nursery tales of *Ka-ni-ga* are of the animals, for the savages associate with the animals on terms of recognized equality; and this is what the prattler in *Ka-ni-ga* says:

The poor little bee
That lives in the tree,
The poor little bee
That lives in the tree,
Has only one arrow
In his quiver.

The arts and industries of savagery and civilization are not in greater contrast than their philosophy. To fully present to you the condition of savagery, as illustrated in their philosophy, three obstacles appear. After all the years I have spent among the Indians in their mountain villages, I am not certain that I have sufficiently divorced myself from the thoughts and ways of civilization to properly appreciate their childish beliefs. The second obstacle subsists in your own knowledge of the methods and powers of nature, and the ways of civilized society; and when I attempt to tell you what an Indian thinks, I fear you will never fully forget what you know, and thus you will be led to give too deep a meaning to a savage explanation; or, on the other hand, contrasting an Indian concept with your own, the manifest absurdity will sound to you as an idle tale too simple to deserve mention, or too false to deserve credence. The third difficulty lies in the attempt to put savage thoughts into civilized language; our words are so full of meaning, carry with them so many great thoughts and collateral ideas.

Some examples of the philosophic methods belonging to widely separated grades of culture may serve to make the previous statements clearer.

Wind.—The *Ute* philosopher discerns that men and animals breathe. He recognizes vaguely the phenomena of the wind, and discovers its resemblance to breath, and explains the winds by relegating them to the class of breathings. He declares that there is a monster beast in the north that breathes the winter winds, and another in the south, and another in the east, and another in the west. The facts relating to winds are but partially discerned; the philosopher has not yet discovered that there is an earth-surrounding atmosphere. He fails in making the proper discriminations. His relegation of the winds to the [Pg 24]class of breathings is analogic, but not homologic. The basis of his philosophy is personality, and hence he has four wind-gods.

The philosopher of the ancient Northland discovered that he could cool his brow with a fan, or kindle a flame, or sweep away the dust with the wafted air. The winds also cooled his brow, the winds also swept away the dust and kindled the fire into a great conflagration, and when the wind blew he said, "Somebody is fanning the waters of the fiord," or "Somebody is fanning the evergreen forests," and he relegated the winds to the class of fannings, and he said, "The god Hræsvelger, clothed with eagle-plumes, is spreading his wings for flight, and the winds rise from under them."

The early Greek philosopher discovered that air may be imprisoned in vessels or move in the ventilation of caves, and he recognized wind as something more than breath, something more than fanning, something that can be gathered up and scattered abroad, and so when the winds blew he said, "The sacks have been untied," or "The caves have been opened."

The philosopher of civilization, has discovered that breath, the fan-wafted breeze, the air confined in vessels, the air moving in ventilation, that these are all parts of the great body of air which surrounds the earth, all in motion, swung by the revolving earth, heated at the tropics, cooled at the poles, and thus turned into counter-currents and again deflected by a thousand geographic features, so that the winds sweep down valleys, eddy among mountain crags, or waft the spray from the crested billows of the sea, all in obedience to cosmic laws. The facts discerned are many, the discriminations made are nice, and the classifications based on true homologies, and we have the science of meteorology, which exhibits an orderly succession of events even in the fickle winds.

Sun and Moon.—The *Ute* philosopher declares the sun to be a living personage, and explains his passage across the heavens along an appointed way by giving an account of a fierce personal conflict between *Tä-vi*, the sun-god, and *Ta-wăts*, one of the supreme gods of his mythology.

In that long ago, the time to which all mythology refers, the sun roamed the earth at will. When he came too near with his fierce heat the people were scorched, and when he hid away in his cave for a long time, too idle to come forth, the night was long and the earth cold. Once upon a time *Ta-wăts*, the hare-god, was sitting with his family by the camp-fire in the solemn woods, anxiously waiting for the return of *Tä-vi*, the wayward sun-god. Wearied with long watching, the hare-god fell asleep, and the sun-god came so near that he scorched the naked shoulder of *Ta-wăts*. Foreseeing the vengeance which would be thus provoked, he fled back to his cave beneath the earth. *Ta-wăts* awoke in great anger, and speedily determined to go and fight the sun-god. After a long journey of many adventures the hare-god came to the brink of the earth, and there watched long and patiently, till at last the sun-god coming out he shot an arrow at his face, but the fierce heat consumed the arrow ere it had finished its intended course; then another arrow was sped, but that was also consumed; and another, and still another, till only one remained in his quiver, but this was the magical arrow that had never failed its mark. *Ta-wăts*, holding it in his hand, lifted the barb to his eye and baptized it in a divine tear; then the arrow was sped and struck the sun-god full in the face, and the sun was shivered into a thousand fragments, which fell to the earth, causing a general conflagration. Then *Ta-wăts*, the hare-god, fled before the destruction he had wrought, and as he fled the burning earth consumed his feet, consumed his legs, consumed his body, consumed his hands and his arms—all were consumed but the head alone, which bowled across valleys and over mountains, fleeing destruction from the burning earth until at last, swollen with heat, the eyes of the god burst and the tears gushed forth in a flood which spread over the earth and extinguished the fire. The sun-god was now conquered, and he appeared before a council of the gods to await sentence. In that long council were established the days and the nights, the seasons and the years, with the length thereof, and the sun was condemned to travel across the firmament by the same trail day after day till the end of time.

In this same philosophy we learn that in that ancient time a council of the gods was held to consider the propriety of making a moon, and at last the task was given to Whippoorwill, a god of the night, and a frog yielded himself a willing sacrifice for this purpose, and the Whippoorwill, by incantations, and other magical means, transformed the frog into the new moon. The truth of this origin of the moon is made evident to our very senses; for do we not see the frog riding the moon at night, and the moon is cold, because the frog from which it was made was cold?

The philosopher of *Oraibi* tells us that when the people ascended by means of the magical tree which constituted the ladder from the lower world to this, they found the firmament, the ceiling of this world, low down upon the earth—the floor of this world, *Matcito*, one of their gods, raised the firmament on his shoulders to where it is now seen. Still the world was dark, as there was no sun, no moon, and no stars. So the people murmured because of the darkness and the cold. *Matcito* said, "Bring me seven maidens," and they brought him seven maidens; and he said, "Bring me seven baskets of cotton-bolls," and they brought him seven baskets of cotton-bolls; and he taught the seven maidens to weave a magical fabric from the cotton, and when they had finished it he held it aloft, and the breeze carried it away toward the firmament, and in the twinkling of an eye it was transformed into a beautiful full-orbed moon, and the same breeze caught the remnants of flocculent cotton which [Pg 26]the maidens had scattered during their work, and carried them aloft, and they were transformed into bright stars. But still it was cold and the people murmured again, and *Matcito* said, "Bring me seven buffalo robes," and they brought him seven buffalo robes, and from the densely matted hair of the robes he wove another wonderful fabric, which the storm carried away into the sky, and it was transformed into the full-orbed sun. Then*Matcito* appointed times and seasons and ways for the heavenly bodies, and the gods of the firmament have obeyed the injunctions of *Matcito* from the day of their creation to the present.

The Norse philosopher tells us that Night and Day, each, has a horse and a car, and they drive successively one after the other around the world in twenty-four hours. Night rides first with her steed named Dew-hair, and every morning as he ends his course he bedews the earth with foam from his bit. The steed driven by Day is Shining-hair. All the sky and earth glisten with the light of his mane. Jarnved, the great iron-wood forest lying to the east of Midgard, is the abode of a race of witches. One monster witch is the mother of many sons in the form of wolves, two of which are Skol and Hate. Skol is the wolf that would devour the maiden Sun, and she daily flies from the maw of the terrible beast, and the moon-man flies from the wolf Hate.

The philosopher of Samos tells us that the earth is surrounded by hollow crystalline spheres set one within another, and all revolving at different rates from east to west about the earth, and that the sun is set in one of these spheres and the moon in another.

The philosopher of civilization tells us that the sun is an incandescent globe, one of the millions afloat in space. About this globe the planets revolve, and the sun and planets and moons were formed from nebulous matter by the gradual segregation of their particles controlled by the laws of gravity, motion, and affinity.

The sun, traveling by an appointed way across the heavens with the never-ending succession of day and night, and the ever-recurring train of seasons, is one of the subjects of every philosophy. Among all peoples, in all times, there is an explanation of these phenomena, but in the lowest stage, way down in savagery, how few the facts discerned, how vague the discriminations made, how superficial the resemblances by which the phenomena are classified! In this stage of culture, all the daily and monthly and yearly phenomena which come as the direct result of the movements of the heavenly bodies are interpreted as the doings of some one—some god acts. In civilization the philosopher presents us the science of astronomy with all its accumulated facts of magnitude, and weights, and orbits, and distances, and velocities—with all the nice discriminations of absolute, relative, and apparent motions; and all these facts he is endeavoring to classify in homologic categories, and the evolutions and revolutions of the heavenly bodies are explained as an orderly succession of events.

[Pg 27]

Rain.—The *Shoshoni* philosopher believes the domed firmament to be ice, and surely it is the very color of ice, and he believes further that a monster serpent-god coils his huge back to the firmament and with his scales abrades its face and causes the ice-dust to fall upon the earth. In the winter-time it falls as snow, but in the summer-time it melts and falls as rain, and the Shoshoni philosopher actually sees the serpent of the storm in the rainbow of many colors.

The *Oraibi* philosopher who lives in a *pueblo* is acquainted with architecture, and so his world is seven-storied. There is a world below and five worlds above this one. *Muiñwa*, the rain-god, who lives in the world immediately above, dips his great brush, made of feathers of the birds of the heavens, into the lakes of the skies and sprinkles the earth with refreshing rain for the irrigation of the crops tilled by these curious Indians who live on the cliffs of Arizona. In winter, *Muiñwa* crushes the ice of the lakes of the heavens and scatters it over the earth, and we have a snow-fall.

The Hindoo philosopher says that the lightning-bearded Indra breaks the vessels that hold the waters of the skies with his thunder-bolts, and the rains descend to irrigate the earth.

The philosopher of civilization expounds to us the methods by which the waters are evaporated from the land and the surface of the sea, and carried away by the winds, and gathered into clouds to be discharged again upon the earth, keeping up forever that wonderful circulation of water from the heavens to the earth and from the earth to the heavens—that orderly succession of events in which the waters travel by river, by sea, and by cloud.

Rainbow.—In *Shoshoni*, the rainbow is a beautiful serpent that abrades the firmament of ice to give us snow and rain. In Norse, the rainbow is the bridge Bifrost spanning the space between heaven and earth. In the Iliad, the rainbow is the goddess Iris, the messenger of the King of Olympus. In Hebrew, the rainbow is the witness to a covenant. In science, the rainbow is an analysis of white light into its constituent colors by the refraction of raindrops.

Falling stars.—In *Ute*, falling stars are the excrements of dirty little star-gods. In science—well, I do not know what falling stars are in science. I think they are cinders from the furnace where the worlds are forged. You may call this mythologic or scientific, as you please.

Migration of birds.—The *Algonkian* philosopher explains the migration of birds by relating the myth of the combat between *Ka-bĭ-bo-no-kĭ* and *Shiñgapis*, the prototype or progenitor of the water-hen, one of their animal gods. A fierce battle raged between *Ka-bĭ-bo-no-kĭ* and *Shiñgapis*, but the latter could not be conquered. All the birds were driven from the land but *Shiñgapis*; and then was it established that whenever in the future Winter-maker should come with his cold winds, fierce snows, and frozen waters, all the birds should leave for the south except *Shiñgapis* and his friends. So the [Pg 28]birds that spend their winters north are called by the *Algonkian* philosophers "the friends of *Shiñgapis*."

In contrast to this explanation of the flight of birds may be placed the explanation of the modern evolutionist, who says that the birds migrate in quest of abundance of food and a genial climate, guided by an instinct of migration, which is an accumulation of inherited memories.

Diversity of languages.—The *Kaibäbĭt* philosopher accounts for the diversity of languages in this manner: *Sĭ-tcom'-pa Ma-só-ĭts*, the grandmother goddess of the sea, brought up mankind from beneath the waves in a sack, which she delivered to the *Cĭn-aú-äv* brothers, the great wolf-gods of his mythology, and told them, to carry it from the shores of the sea to the Kaibab Plateau, and then to open it; but they were by no means to open the package ere their arrival, lest some great disaster should befall. The curiosity of the younger*Cĭn-aú-äv* overcame him, and he untied the sack, and the people swarmed out; but the elder *Cĭn-aú-äv*, the wiser god, ran back and closed the sack while yet not all the people had escaped, and they carried the sack, with its remaining contents, to the plateau, and there opened it. Those that remained in the sack found a beautiful land—a great plateau covered with mighty forests, through which elk, deer, and antelope roamed in abundance, and many mountain-sheep were found on the bordering crags; *piv*, the nuts of the edible pine, they found on the foot-hills, and *us*, the fruit of the yucca, in sunny glades; and *nänt*, the meschal crowns, for their feasts; and *tcu-ar*, the cactus-apple, from which to make their wine; reeds grew about the lakes for their arrow-shafts; the rocks were full of flints for their barbs and knives, and away down, in the cañon they found a pipe-stone quarry, and on the hills they found *är-a-ûm-pĭv*, their tobacco. O, it was a beautiful land that was given to these, the favorites of the gods! The descendants of these people are the present *Kaibäbĭts* of northern Arizona. Those who escaped by the way, through the wicked curiosity of the younger *Cĭn-aú-äv*, scattered over the country and became *Navajos, Mokis, Sioux, Comanches,* Spaniards, Americans—poor, sorry fragments of people without the original language of the gods, and only able to talk in imperfect jargons.

The Hebrew philosopher tells us that on the plains of Shinar the people of the world were gathered to build a city and erect a tower, the summit of which should reach above the waves of any flood Jehovah might send. But their tongues were confused as a punishment for their impiety. The philosopher of science tells us that mankind was widely scattered over the earth anterior to the development of articulate speech, that the languages of which we are cognizant sprang from innumerable centers as each little tribe developed its own language, and that in the study of any language an orderly succession of events may be discovered in its evolution from a few simple holophrastic locutions to a complex language with a multiplicity of words and an elaborate grammatic structure, by the differentiation of the parts of speech and the integration of the [Pg 29]sentence.

A cough.—A man coughs. In explanation the *Ute* philosopher would tell us that an *u-nú-pĭts*—a pygmy spirit of evil—had entered the poor man's stomach, and he would charge the invalid with having whistled at night; for in their philosophy it is taught that if a man whistles at night, when the pygmy spirits are abroad, one is sure to go through the open door into the stomach, and the evidence of this disaster is found in the cough which the *u-nú-pĭts* causes. Then the evil spirit must be driven out, and the medicine-man stretches his patient on the ground and scarifies him with the claws of eagles from head to heel, and while performing the scarification a group of men and women stand about, forming a chorus, and medicine-man and chorus perform a fugue in gloomy ululation, for these wicked spirits will depart only by incantations and scarifications.

In our folk-lore philosophy a cough is caused by a "cold," whatever that may be—a vague entity—that must be treated first according to the maxim "Feed a cold and starve a fever," and the "cold" is driven away by potations of bitter teas.

In our medical philosophy a cough may be the result of a clogging of the pores of the skin, and is relieved by clearing those flues that carry away the waste products of vital combustion.

These illustrations are perhaps sufficient to exhibit the principal characteristics of the two methods of philosophy, and, though they cover but narrow fields, it should be remembered that every philosophy deals with the whole cosmos. An explanation of all things is sought—not alone the great movements of the heavens, or the phenomena that startle even the unthinking, but every particular which is observed. Abstractly, the plane of demarkation between the two methods of philosophy can be sharply drawn, but practically we find them strangely mixed; mythologic methods prevail in savagery and barbarism, and scientific methods prevail in civilization. Mythologic philosophies antedate scientific philosophies. The thaumaturgic phases of mythology are the embryonic stages of philosophy, science being the fully developed form. Without mythology there could be no science, as without childhood there could be no manhood, or without embryonic conditions there could be no ultimate forms.

MYTHOLOGIC PHILOSOPHY HAS FOUR STAGES.

Mythologic philosophy is the subject with which we deal. Its method, as stated in general terms, is this: All phenomena of the outer objective world are interpreted by comparison with those of the inner subjective world Whatever happens, some one does it; that some one has a will and works as he wills. The basis of the philosophy is personality. The persons who do the things which we observe in the phenomena of the [Pg 30]universe are the gods of mythology—*the cosmos is a pantheon*. Under this system, whatever may be the phenomenon observed, the philosopher asks, "Who does it?" and "Why?" and the answer comes, "A god with his design." The winds blow, and the interrogatory is answered, "Æolus frees them from the cave to speed the ship of a friend, or destroy the vessel of a foe." The actors in mythologic philosophy are gods.

In the character of these gods four stages of philosophy may be discovered. In the lowest and earliest stage everything has life; everything is endowed with personality, will, and design; animals are endowed with all the wonderful attributes of mankind; all inanimate objects are believed to be animate; trees think and speak; stones have loves and hates; hills and mountains, springs and rivers, and all the bright stars, have life—everything discovered objectively by the senses is looked upon subjectively by the philosopher and endowed with all the attributes supposed to be inherent in himself. In this stage of philosophy everything is a god. Let us call it *hecastotheism*.

In the second stage men no longer attribute life indiscriminately to inanimate things; but the same powers and attributes recognized by subjective vision in man are attributed to the animals by which he is surrounded. No line of demarkation is drawn between man and beast; all are great beings endowed with wonderful attributes. Let us call this stage *zoötheism*, when men worship beasts. All the phenomena of nature are the doings of these animal gods; all the facts of nature, all the phenomena of the known universe, all the institutions of humanity known to the philosophers of this stage, are accounted for in the mythologic history of these zoömorphic gods.

In the third stage a wide gulf is placed between man and the lower animals. The animal gods are dethroned, and the powers and phenomena of nature are personified and deified. Let us call this stage *physitheism*. The gods are strictly anthropomorphic, having the form as well as the mental, moral, and social attributes of men. Thus we have a god of the sun, a god of the moon, a god of the air, a god of dawn, and a deity of the night.

In the fourth stage, mental, moral, and social characteristics are personified and deified. Thus we have a god of war, a god of love, a god of revelry, a god of plenty, and like personages who preside over the institutions and occupations of mankind. Let us call this *psychotheism*. With the mental, moral, and social characteristics in these gods are associated the powers of nature; and they differ from nature-gods chiefly in that they have more distinct psychic characteristics.

Psychotheism, by the processes of mental integration, develops in one direction into monotheism, and in the other into pantheism. When the powers of nature are held predominant in the minds of the philosophers through whose cogitations this evolution of theism is carried on, pantheism, as the highest form of psychotheism, is the final result; but when the moral qualities are held in highest regard in the minds of the men in whom this process of evolution is carried on, *monotheism*, or a [Pg 31]god whose essential characteristics are moral qualities, is the final product. The monotheistic god is not nature, but presides over and operates through, nature. Psychotheism has long been recognized. All of the earlier literature of mankind treats largely of these gods, for it is an interesting fact that in the history of any civilized people, the evolution of psychotheism is approximately synchronous with the invention of an alphabet. In the earliest writings of the Egyptians, the Hindoos, and the Greeks, this stage is discovered, and Osiris, Indra, and Zeus are characteristic representatives. As psychotheism and written language appear together in the evolution of culture, this stage of theism is consciously or unconsciously a part of the theme of all written history.

The paleontologist, in studying the rocks of the hill and the cliffs of the mountain, discovers, in inanimate stones, the life-forms of the ancient earth. The geologist, in the study of the structure of valleys and mountains, discovers groups of facts that lead him to a knowledge of more ancient mountains and valleys and seas, of geographic features long ago buried, and followed by a new land with new mountains and valleys, and new seas. The philologist, in studying the earliest writings of a people, not only discovers the thoughts purposely recorded in those writings, but is able to go back in the history of the people many generations, and discover with even greater certainty the thoughts of the more ancient people who made the words. Thus the writings of the Greeks, the Hindoos, and the Egyptians, that give an account of their psychic gods, also contain a description of an earlier theism unconsciously recorded by the writers themselves. Psychotheism prevailed when the sentences were coined, physitheism when the words were coined. So the philologist discovers physitheism in all ancient literature. But the verity of that stage of philosophy does not rest alone upon the evidence derived from the study of fossil philosophies through the science of philology. In the folk-lore of every civilized people having a psychotheistic philosophy, an earlier philosophy with nature-gods is discovered.

The different stages of philosophy which I have attempted to characterize have never been found in purity. We always observe different methods of explanation existing side by side, and the type of a philosophy is determined by the prevailing characteristics of its explanation of phenomena. Fragments of the earlier are always found side by side with, the greater body of the later philosophy. Man has never clothed himself in new garments of wisdom, but has ever been patching the old, and the old and the new are blended in the same pattern, and thus we have atavism in philosophy. So in the study of any philosophy which has reached the psychotheistic age, patches of the earlier philosophy are always seen. Ancient nature-gods are found to be living and associating with the supreme psychic deities. Thus in anthropologic science there are three ways by which, to go back in the history of any civilized people and learn of its barbaric physitheism. But of the verity of this stage we have further evidence. When Christianity was [Pg 32]carried north from Central Europe, the champions of the new philosophy, and its consequent religion, discovered, among those who dwelt by the glaciers of the north, a barbaric philosophy which they have preserved to history in the Eddas and Sagas, and Norse literature is full of a philosophy in a transition state, from physitheism to psychotheism; and, mark! the people discovered in this transition state were inventing an alphabet—they were carving Runes. Then a pure physitheism was discovered in the Aztec barbarism of Mexico; and elsewhere on the globe many people were found in that stage of culture to which this philosophy properly belongs. Thus the existence of physitheism as a stage of philosophy is abundantly attested. Comparative mythologists are agreed in recognizing these two stages. They might not agree to throw all of the higher and later philosophies into one group, as I have done, but all recognize the plane of demarkation between the higher and the lower groups as I have drawn it. Scholars, too, have come essentially to an agreement that physitheism is earlier and older than psychotheism. Perhaps there may be left a "doubting Thomas" who believes that the highest stage of psychotheism—that is, monotheism—was the original basis for the philosophy of the world, and that all other forms are degeneracies from that primitive and perfect state. If there be such a man left, to him what I have to say about philosophy is blasphemy.

Again, all students of comparative philosophy, or comparative mythology, or comparative religion, as you may please to approach this subject from different points of view, recognize that there is something else; that there are philosophies, or mythologies, or religions, not included in the two great groups. All that something else has been vaguely called fetichism. I have divided it into two parts, *hecastotheism* and *zoötheism*. The verity of zoötheism as a stage of philosophy rests on abundant evidence. In psychotheism it appears as *devilism* in obedience to a well-known law of comparative theology, viz, that the gods of a lower and superseded stage of culture oftentimes become the devils of a higher stage. So in the very highest stages of psychotheism we find beast-devils. In Norse mythology, we have Fenris the wolf, and Jormungandur the serpent. Dragons appear in Greek mythology, the bull is an Egyptian god, a serpent is found in the Zendavesta; and was there not a scaly fellow in the garden of Eden? So common are these beast-demons in the higher mythologies that they are used in every literature as rhetorical figures. So we find, as a figure of speech, the great red dragon with seven heads and ten horns, with tail that with one brush sweeps away a third of the stars of heaven. And where-ever we find nature-worship we find it accompanied with beast-worship. In the study of higher philosophies, having learned that lower philosophies often exist side by side with them, we might legitimately conclude that a philosophy based upon animal gods had existed previous to the development of physitheism; and philologic research, leads to the same [Pg 33]conclusion. But we are not left to base this conclusion upon, an induction only, for in the examination of savage philosophies we actually discover zoötheism in all its proportions. Many of the Indians of North America, and many of South America, and many of the tribes of Africa, are found to be zoötheists. Their supreme gods are animals—tigers, bears, wolves, serpents, birds. Having discovered this, with a vast accumulation of evidence, we are enabled to carry philosophy back one stage beyond physitheism, and we can confidently assert that all the philosophies of civilization have come up through these three stages.

And yet, there are fragments of philosophy discovered which are not zoötheistic, physitheistic, nor psychotheistic. What are they? We find running through all three stages of higher philosophy that phenomena are sometimes explained by regarding them as the acts of persons who do not belong to any of the classes of gods found in the higher stages. We find fragments of philosophy everywhere which seem to assume that all inanimate nature is animate; that mountains and hills, and rivers and springs, that trees and grasses, that stones, and all fragments of things are endowed with life and with will, and act for a purpose. These fragments of philosophy lead to the discovery of hecastotheism. Philology also leads us back to that state when the animate and the inanimate were confounded, for the holophrastic roots into which words are finally resolved show us that all inanimate things were represented in language as actors. Such is the evidence on which we predicate the existence of hecastotheism as a veritable stage of philosophy. Unlike the three higher stages, it has no people extant on the face of the globe, known to be in this stage of culture. The philosophies of many of the lowest tribes of mankind are yet unknown, and hecastotheism may be discovered; but at the present time we are not warranted in saying that any tribe entertains this philosophy as its highest wisdom.

OUTGROWTH FROM MYTHOLOGIC PHILOSOPHY.

The three stages of mythologic philosophy that are still extant in the world must be more thoroughly characterized, and the course of their evolution indicated. But in order to do this clearly, certain outgrowths from mythologic philosophy must be explained—certain theories and practices that necessarily result from, this philosophy, and that are intricately woven into the institutions of mankind.

Ancientism.—The first I denominate ancientism. Yesterday was better than to-day. The ancients were wiser that we. This belief in a better day and a better people in the elder time is almost universal among mankind. A belief so widely spread, so profoundly entertained, must have for its origin some important facts in the constitution or history of [Pg 34]mankind. Let us see what they are.

In the history of every individual the sports and joys of childhood are compared and contrasted with the toils and pains of old age. Greatly protracted life, in savagery and barbarism, is not a boon to be craved. In that stage of society where the days and the years go by with little or no provision for a time other than that which is passing, the old must go down to the grave through poverty and suffering. In that stage of culture to-morrow's bread is not certain, and to-day's bread is often scarce. In civilization plenty and poverty live side by side; the palace and the hovel are on the same landscape; the rich and poor elbow each other on the same street; but in savagery plenty and poverty come with recurring days to the same man, and the tribe is rich to-day and poor to-morrow, and the days of want come in every man's history; and when they come the old suffer most, and the burden of old age is oppressive. In youth activity is joy; in old age activity is pain. So wonder, then, that old age loves youth, or that to-day loves yesterday, for the instinct is born of the inherited experiences of mankind.

But there is yet another and more potent reason for ancientism. That tale is the most wonderful that has been most repeated, for the breath of speech is the fertilizer of story. Hence, the older the story the greater its thaumaturgics. Thus, yesterday is greater than to-day by natural processes of human exaggeration. Again, that is held to be most certain, and hence most sacred, which has been most often affirmed. A Brahman was carrying a goat to the altar. Three thieves would steal it. So they placed themselves at intervals along the way by which the pious Brahman would travel. When the venerable man came to the first thief he was accosted: "Brahman, why do you carry a dog?" Now, a dog is an unclean beast which no Brahman must touch. And the Brahman, after looking at his goat, said: "You do err; this is a goat." And when the old man reached the second thief, again he was accosted: "Brahman, why do you carry a dog?" So the Brahman put his goat on the ground, and after narrowly scrutinizing it, he said: "Surely this is a goat," and went on his way. When he came to the third thief he was once more accosted: "Brahman, why do you carry a dog?" Then the Brahman, having thrice heard that his goat was a dog, was convinced, and throwing it down, he fled to the temple for ablution, and the thieves had a feast.

The child learns not for himself, but is taught, and accepts as true that which is told, and a propensity to believe the affirmed is implanted in his mind. In every society some are wise and some are foolish, and the wise are revered, and their affirmations are accepted. Thus, the few lead the multitude in knowledge, and the propensity to believe the affirmed started in childhood is increased in manhood in the great average of persons constituting society, and these propensities are inherited from generation to generation, until we have a cumulation of effects.

The propagation of opinions by affirmation, the cultivation of the propensity to believe that which has been affirmed many times, let us [Pg 35]call *affirmatization*. If the world's opinions were governed only by the principles of mythologic philosophy, affirmatization would become so powerful that nothing would be believed but the anciently affirmed. Men would come to no new knowledge. Society would stand still listening to the wisdom of the fathers. But the power of affirmatization is steadily undermined by science.

And, still again, the institutions of society conform to its philosophy. The explanations of things always includes the origin of human institutions. So the welfare of society is based on philosophy, and the venerable sayings which constitute philosophy are thus held as sacred. So ancientism is developed from accumulated life-experiences; by the growth of story in repeated narration; by the steadily increasing power of affirmatization, and by respect for the authority upon which the institutions of society are based; all accumulating as they come down the generations. That we do thus inherit effects we know, for has it not been affirmed in the Book that "the fathers have eaten grapes, and the children's teeth are set on edge"? As men come to believe that the "long ago" was better than the "now," and the dead were better than the living, then philosophy must necessarily include a theory of degeneracy, which is a part of ancientism.

Theistic Society.—Again, the actors in mythologic philosophy are personages, and we always find them organized in societies. The social organization of mythology is always found to be essentially identical with the social organization of the people who entertain the philosophy. The gods are husbands and wives, and parents and children, and the gods have an organized government. This gives us theistic society, and we cannot properly characterize a theism without taking its mythic society into consideration.

Spiritism.—In the earliest stages of society of which we have practical knowledge by acquaintance with the people themselves, a belief in the existence of spirits prevails—a shade, an immaterial existence, which is the duplicate of the material personage. The genesis of this belief is complex. The workings of the human mind during periods of unconsciousness lead to opinions that are enforced by many physical phenomena.

First, we have the activities of the mind during sleep, when the man seems to go out from himself, to converse with his friends, to witness strange scenes, and to have many wonderful experiences. Thus the man seems to have lived an eventful life, when his body was, in fact, quiescent and unconscious. Memories of scenes and activities in former days, and the inherited memories of scenes witnessed and actions performed by ancestors, are blended in strange confusion by broken and inverted sequences. Now and then the dream-scenes are enacted in real life, and the infrequent coincidence or apparent verification makes deep impression on the mind, while unfulfilled dreams are forgotten. Thus the [Pg 36]dreams of sleepers are attributed to their immaterial duplicates their spirits. In many diseases, also, the mind seems to wander, to see sights and to hear sounds, and to have many wonderful experiences, while the body itself is apparently unconscious. Sometimes, on restored health, the person may recall these wonderful experiences, and during their occurrence the subject talks to unseen persons, and seems to have replies, and to act, to those who witness, in such a manner that a second self—a spirit independent of the body—is suggested. When disease amounts to long-continued insanity all of these effects are greatly exaggerated, and make a deep impression upon all who witness the phenomena. Thus the hallucinations of fever-racked brains, and mad minds, are attributed to spirits.

The same conditions of apparent severance of mind and body witnessed in dreams and hallucinations are often produced artificially in the practice of *ecstasism*. In the vicissitudes of savage life, while little or no provision is made for the future, there are times when the savage resorts to almost anything at hand as a means of subsistence, and thus all plants and all parts of plants, seed, fruit, flowers, leaves, bark, roots—anything in times of extreme want—may be used as food. But experience soon teaches the various effects upon the human system which are produced by the several vegetable substances with which he meets, and thus the effect of narcotics is early discovered, and the savage in the practice of his religion oftentimes resorts to these native drugs for the purpose of producing an ecstatic state under which divination may be performed. The practice of ecstasism is universal in the lower stages of culture. In times of great anxiety, every savage and barbarian seeks to know of the future.

Through all the earlier generations of mankind, ecstasism has been practiced, and civilized man has thus an inherited appetite for narcotics, to which the enormous propensity to drunkenness existing in all nations bears witness. When the great actor in his personation of Rip Van Winkle holds his goblet aloft and says, "Here's to your health and to your family's, and may they live long and prosper," he connects the act of drinking with a prayer, and unconsciously demonstrates the origin of the use of stimulants. It may be that when the jolly companion has become a loathsome sot, and his mind is ablaze with the fire of drink, and he sees uncouth beasts in horrid presence, that inherited memories haunt him with visions of the beast-gods worshipped by his ancestors at the very time when the appetite for stimulants was created.

But ecstasism is produced in other ways, and for this purpose the savage and barbarian often resorts to fasting and bodily torture. In many ways he produces the wonderful state, and the visions of ecstasy are interpreted as the evidence of spirits.

Many physical phenomena serve to confirm this opinion. It is very late in philosophy when shadows are referred to the interception of the rays of the sun. In savagery and barbarism, shadows are supposed to be emanations from or duplicates of the bodies causing the shadows. And [Pg 37]what savage understands the reflection of the rays of the sun by which images are produced? They also are supposed to be emanations or duplications of the object reflected. No savage or barbarian could understand that the waves of the air are turned back, and sound is duplicated in an echo. He knows not that there is an atmosphere, and to him the echo is the voice of an unseen, personage—a spirit. There is no theory more profoundly implanted in early mankind than that of spiritism.

Thaumaturgics.—The gods of mythologic philosophies are created to account for the wonders of nature. Necessarily they are a wonder-working folk, and, having been endowed with these magical powers in all the histories given in mythic tales of their doings on the earth, we find them performing most wonderful feats. They can transform themselves; they can disappear and reappear; all their senses are magical; some are endowed with a multiplicity of eyes, others have a multiplicity of ears; in Norse mythology the watchman on the rainbow bridge could hear the grass grow, and wool on the backs of sheep; arms can stretch out to grasp the distance, tails can coil about mountains, and all powers become magical. But the most wonderful power with which the gods are endowed is the power of will, for we find that they can think their arrows to the hearts of their enemies; mountains are overthrown by thought, and thoughts are projected into other minds. Such are the thaumaturgics of mythologic philosophy.

Mythic tales.—Early man having created through the development of his philosophy a host of personages, these gods must have a history. A part of that history, and the most important part to us as students of philosophy, is created in the very act of creating the gods themselves. I mean that portion of their history which relates to the operations of nature, for the gods were created to account for those things. But to this is added much else of adventure. The gods love as men love, and go in quest of mates. The gods hate as men hate, and fight in single combat or engage in mythic battles; and the history of these adventures impelled by love and hate, and all other passions and purposes with which men are endowed, all woven into a complex tissue with their doings in carrying out the operations of nature, constitutes the web and woof of mythology.

Religion.—Again, as human welfare is deeply involved in the operations of nature, man's chief interest is in the gods. In this interest religion originates. Man, impelled by his own volition, guided by his own purposes, aspires to a greater happiness, and endeavor follows endeavor, but at every step his progress is impeded; his own powers fail before the greater powers of nature; his powers are pygmies, nature's powers are giants, and to him these giants are gods with wills and purposes of their own, and he sees that man in his weakness can succeed only by allying himself with the gods. Hence, impelled by this philosophy, man must have communion with the gods, and in this communion [Pg 38]he must influence them to work for himself. Hence, religion, which has to do with the relations which exist between the gods and man, is the legitimate offspring of mythologic philosophy.

Thus we see that out of mythologic philosophy, as branches of the great tree itself, there grow ancientism, theistic society, spiritism, thaumaturgics, mythic tales, and religion.

THE COURSE OF EVOLUTION IN MYTHOLOGIC PHILOSOPHY.

I shall now give a summary characterization of zoötheism, then call attention to some of the relics of hecastotheism found therein, and proceed with a brief statement of the higher stages of theism. The apparent and easily accessible is studied first. In botany, the trees and the conspicuous flowering plants of garden, field, and plain were first known, and then all other plants were vaguely grouped as weeds; but, since the most conspicuous phenogamous plants were first studied, what vast numbers of new orders, new genera, and new species have been discovered, in the progress of research, to the lowest cryptogams!

In the study of ethnology we first recognized the more civilized races. The Aryan, Hamites, Shemites, and Chinese, and the rest were the weeds of humanity—the barbarian and savage, sometimes called Turanians. But, when we come carefully to study these lower people, what numbers of races are discovered! In North America alone we have more than seventy-five—seventy-five stocks of people speaking seventy-five stocks of language, and some single stocks embracing many distinct languages and dialects. The languages of the Algonkian family are as diverse as the Indo-European tongues. So are the languages of the Dakotans, the Shoshonians, the Tinnéans, and others; so that in North America we have more than five hundred languages spoken to-day. Each linguistic stock is found to have a philosophy of its own, and each stock as many branches of philosophy as it has languages and dialects. North America presents a magnificent field for the study of savage and barbaric philosophies.

This vast region of thought has been explored only by a few adventurous travelers in the world of science. No thorough survey of any part has been made. Yet the general outlines of North American philosophy are known, but the exact positions, the details, are all yet to be filled in—as the geography of the general outline of North America is known by exploration, but the exact positions and details of topography are yet to be filled in as the result of careful survey. Myths of the Algonkian stock are found in many a volume of *Americana*, the best of which were recorded by the early missionaries who came from Europe, though we find some of them, mixed with turbid speculations, in the writings of[Pg 39]Schoolcraft. Many of the myths of the Indians of the south, in that region stretching back from the great Gulf, are known; some collected by travelers, others by educated Indians.

Many of the myths of the Iroquois are known. The best of these are in the writings of Morgan, America's greatest anthropologist. Missionaries, travelers, and linguists have given us a great store of the myths of the Dakotan stock. Many myths of the Tinnéan also have been collected. Petitot has recorded a number of those found at the north, and we have in manuscript some of the myths of a southern branch—the Navajos. Perhaps the myths of the Shoshonians have been collected more thoroughly than those of any other stock. These are yet unpublished, but the manuscripts are in the library of the Bureau of Ethnology. Powers has recorded many of the myths of various stocks in California, and the old Spanish writings give us a fair collection of the Nahuatlan myths of Mexico, and Rink has presented an interesting volume on the mythology of the Innuits; and, finally, fragments of mythology have been collected from nearly all the tribes of North America, and they are scattered through thousands of volumes, so that the literature is vast. The brief description which I shall give of zoötheism is founded on a study of the materials which I have thus indicated.

All these tribes are found in the higher stages of savagery, or the lower stages of barbarism, and their mythologies are found to be zoötheistic among the lowest, physitheistic among the highest, and a great number of tribes are found in a transition state: for zoötheism is found to be a characteristic of savagery, and physitheism of barbarism, using the terms as they have been defined by Morgan. The supreme gods of this stage are animals. The savage is intimately associated with animals. From them he obtains the larger part of his clothing, and much of his food, and he carefully studies their habits and finds many wonderful things. Their knowledge and skill and power appear to him to be superior to his own. He sees the mountain-sheep fleet among the crags, the eagle soaring in the heavens, the humming-bird poised over its blossom-cup of nectar, the serpents swift without legs, the salmon scaling the rapids, the spider weaving its gossamer web, the ant building a play-house mountain—in all animal nature he sees things too wonderful for him, and from admiration he grows to adoration, and the animals become his gods.

Ancientism plays an important part in this zoötheism. It is not the animals of to-day whom the Indians worship, but their progenitors—their prototypes. The wolf of to-day is a howling pest, but that wolf's ancestor—the first of the line—was a god. The individuals of every species are supposed to have descended from an ancient being—a progenitor of the race; and so they have a grizzly-bear god, an eagle-god, a rattlesnake-god, a trout-god, a spider-god—a god for every species and variety of animal.

By these animal gods all things were established. The heavenly bodies [Pg 40] were created and their ways appointed, and when the powers and phenomena of nature are personified the personages are beasts, and all human institutions also were established by the ancient animal-gods.

The ancient animals of any philosophy of this stage are found to constitute a clan or *gens*—a body of relatives, or *consanguinei* with grandfathers, fathers, sons, and brothers. In *Ute* theism, the ancient *To-gó-äv*, the first rattlesnake is the grandfather, and all the animal-gods are assigned to their relationships. Grandfather *To-gó-äv*, the wise, was the chief of the council, but *Cĭn-aú-äv*, the ancient wolf, was the chief of the clan.

There were many other clans and tribes of ancient gods with whom these supreme gods had dealings, of which hereafter; and, finally, each of these ancient gods became the progenitor of a new tribe, so that we have a tribe of bears, a tribe of eagles, a tribe of rattlesnakes, a tribe of spiders, and many other tribes, as we have tribes of Utes, tribes of Sioux, tribes of Navajos; and in that philosophy tribes of animals are considered to be coördinate with tribes of men. All of these gods have invisible duplicates—spirits—and they have often visited the earth. All of the wonderful things seen in nature are done by the animal-gods. That elder life was a magic life; but the descendants of the gods are degenerate. Now and then as a medicine-man by practicing sorcery can perform great feats, so now and then there is a medicine-bear, a medicine-wolf, or a medicine-snake that can work magic.

On winter nights the Indians gather about the camp-fire, and then the doings of the gods are recounted in many a mythic tale. I have heard the venerable and impassioned orator on the camp-meeting stand rehearse the story of the crucifixion, and have seen the thousands gathered there weep in contemplation of the story of divine suffering, and heard their shouts roll down the forest aisles as they gave vent to their joy at the contemplation of redemption. But the scene was not a whit more dramatic than another I have witnessed in an evergreen forest of the Rocky Mountain region, where a tribe was gathered under the great pines, and the temple of light from the blazing fire was walled by the darkness of midnight, and in the midst of the temple stood the wise old man, telling, in simple savage language, the story of *Ta-wăts*, when he conquered the sun and established the seasons and the days. In that pre-Columbian time, before the advent of white men, all the Indian tribes of North America gathered on winter nights by the shores of the seas where the tides beat in solemn rhythm, by the shores of the great lakes where the waves dashed against frozen beaches, and by the banks of the rivers flowing ever in solemn mystery—each in its own temple of illumined space—and listened to the story of its own supreme gods, the ancients of time.

Religion, in this stage of theism, is sorcery. Incantation, dancing, fasting, bodily torture, and ecstasism are practiced. Every tribe has its potion or vegetable drug, by which the ecstatic state is produced, and their venerable medicine-men see visions and dream dreams. No [Pg 41]enterprise is undertaken without consulting the gods, and no evil impends but they seek to propitiate the gods. All daily life, to the minutest particular, is religious. This stage of religion is characterized by fetichism. Every Indian is provided with his charm or fetich, revealed to him in some awful hour of ecstasy produced by fasting, or feasting, or drunkenness, and that fetich he carries with him to bring good luck, in love or in combat, in the hunt or on the journey. He carries a fetich suspended to his neck, he ties a fetich to his bow, he buries a fetich under his tent, he places a fetich under his pillow of wild-cat skins, he prays to his fetich, he praises it, or chides it; if successful, his fetich receives glory; if he fail, his fetich is disgraced. These fetiches may be fragments of bone or shell, the tips of the tails of animals, the claws of birds or beasts, perhaps dried hearts of little warblers, shards of beetles, leaves powdered and held in bags, or crystals from the rocks—anything curious may become a fetich. Fetichism, then, is a religious means, not a philosophic or mythologic state. Such are the supreme gods of the savage, and such the institutions which belong to their theism. But they have many other inferior gods. Mountains, hills, valleys, and great rocks have their own special deities—invisible spirits—and lakes, rivers, and springs are the homes of spirits. But all these have animal forms when in proper *personæ*. Yet some of the medicine-spirits can transform themselves, and work magic as do medicine-men. The heavenly bodies are either created personages or ancient men or animals translated to the sky. And, last, we find that ancestors are worshipped as gods.

Among all the tribes of North America with which we are acquainted tutelarism prevails. Every tribe and every clan has its own protecting god, and every individual has his *my god*. It is a curious fact that every Indian seeks to conceal the knowledge of his *my god* from all other persons, for he fears that, if his enemy should know of his tutelar deity, he might by extraordinary magic succeed in estranging him, and be able to compass his destruction through his own god.

In this summary characterization of zoötheism, I have necessarily systematized my statements. This, of course, could not be done by the savage himself. He could give you its particulars, but could not group those particulars in any logical way. He does not recognize any system, but talks indiscriminately, now of one, now of another god, and with him the whole theory as a system is vague and shadowy, but its particulars are vividly before his mind, and the certainty with which he entertains his opinions leaves no room to doubt his sincerity.

But there is yet another phase of theism discovered. Sometimes a particular mountain, or hill, or some great rock, some waterfall, some lake, or some spring receives special worship, and is itself believed to be a deity. This seems to be a relic of hecastotheism. Fetichism, also, seems to have come from that lower grade, and all the minor deities, the spirits of mountains and hills and forest, seem to have been derived from that same stage, but with this development, that the things [Pg 42]themselves are not worshipped, but their essential spirits.

From zoötheism, as described, to physitheism the way is long. Gradually, in the progress of philosophy, animal gods are dethroned and become inferior gods or are forgotten; and gradually the gods of the firmament—the sun, the moon, the stars—are advanced to supremacy; the clouds, the storms, the winds, day and night, dawn and gloaming, the sky, the earth, the sea, and all the various phases of nature perceived by the barbaric mind, are personified and deified and exalted to a supremacy coordinate with the firmament gods; and all the gods of the lower stage that remain—animals, demons, and all men—belong to inferior tribes. The gods of the sky—the shining ones, those that soar on bright wings, those that are clothed in gorgeous colors, those that came from we know not where, those that vanish to the unknown—are the supreme gods. We always find these gods organized in great tribes, with mighty chieftains who fight in great combats or lead their hosts in battle, and return with much booty. Such is the theism of ancient Mexico, such the theism of the Northland, and such the theism discovered among the ancient Aryans.

From this stage to psychotheism the way is long, for evolution is slow. Gradually men come to differentiate more carefully between good and evil, and the ethic character of their gods becomes the subject of consideration, and the good gods grow in virtue, and the bad gods grow in vice. Their identity with physical objects and phenomena is gradually lost. The different phases or conditions of the same object or phenomenon are severed, and each is personified. The bad gods are banished to underground homes, or live in concealment, from which they issue on their expeditions of evil. Still, all powers exist in these gods, and all things were established by them. With the growth of their moral qualities no physical powers are lost, and the sports of the physical bodies and phenomena become demons, subordinate to the great gods who preside over nature and human institutions.

We find, also, that these superior gods are organized in societies. I have said the Norse mythology was in a transition state from physitheism to psychotheism. The Asas, or gods, lived in Asgard, a mythic communal village, with its Thing or Council, the very counterpart of the communal village of Iceland. Olympus was a Greek city.

Still further in the study of mythologic philosophy we see that more and more supremacy falls into the hands of the few, until monotheism is established on the plan of the empire. Then all of the inferior deities whose characters are pure become ministering angels, and the inferior deities whose characters are evil become devils, and the differentiation of good and evil is perfected in the gulf between heaven and hell. In all this time from zoötheism to monotheism, ancientism becomes more ancient, and the times and dynasties are multiplied. Spiritism is more clearly defined, and spirits become eternal; mythologic tales are codified, and sacred books are written; divination for the result of amorous intrigue has become the prophecy of immortality, and [Pg 43]thaumaturgics is formulated as the omnipresent, the omnipotent, the omniscient—the infinite.

Time has failed me to tell of the evolution of idolatry from fetichism, priestcraft from sorcery, and of their overthrow by the doctrines that were uttered by that voice on the Mount. Religion, that was fetichism and ecstasism and sorcery, is now the yearning for something better, something purer, and the means by which this highest state for humanity may be reached, the ideal worship of the highest monotheism, is "in spirit and in truth." The steps are long from *Cĭn-aú-äv*, the ancient of wolves, by Zeus, the ancient of skies, to Jehovah, the "Ancient of Days."

MYTHIC TALES.

In every Indian tribe there is a great body of story lore—tales purporting to be the sayings and doings, the history, of the gods. Every tribe has one or more persons skilled in the relation of these stories—preachers. The long winter evenings are set apart for this purpose. Then the men and women, the boys and girls, gather about the camp-fire to listen to the history of the ancients, to a chapter in the unwritten bible of savagery. Such a scene is of the deepest interest. A camp-fire of blazing pine or sage boughs illumines a group of dusky faces intent with expectation, and the old man begins his story, talking and acting; the elders receiving his words with reverence, while the younger persons are played upon by the actor until they shiver with fear or dance with delight. An Indian is a great actor. The conditions of Indian life train them in natural sign language. Among the two hundred and fifty or three hundred thousand Indians in the United States, there are scores of languages, so that often a language is spoken by only a few hundred or a few score of people; and as a means of communication between tribes speaking different languages, a sign language has grown up, so that an Indian is able to talk all over—with the features of his face, his hands and feet, the muscles of his body; and thus a skillful preacher talks and acts; and, inspired by a theme which treats of the gods, he sways his savage audience at will. And ever as he tells his story he points a moral—the mythology, theology, religion, history, and all human duties are taught. This preaching is one of the most important institutions of savagery. The whole body of myths current in a tribe is the sum total of their lore—their philosophy, their miraculous history, their authority for their governmental institutions, their social[Pg 44]institutions, their habits and customs. It is their unwritten bible.

THE CĬN-AÚ-ÄV BROTHERS DISCUSS MATTERS OF IMPORTANCE TO THE PEOPLE.

Once upon a time the *Cĭn-aú-äv* brothers met to consult about the destiny of the *U-ĭn-ká-rĕts*. At this meeting the younger said: "Brother, how shall these people obtain their food? Let us devise some good plan for them. I was thinking about it all night, but could not see what would be best, and when the dawn came into the sky I went to a mountain and sat on its summit, and thought a long time; and now I can tell you a good plan by which they can live. Listen to your younger brother. Look at these pine trees; their nuts are sweet; and there is the *us*, very rich; and there is the apple of the cactus, full of juice; on the plain you see the sunflower, bearing many seeds—they will be good for the nation. Let them have all these things for their food, and when they have gathered a store they shall put them in the ground, or hide them in the rocks, and when they return they shall find abundance, and having taken of them as they may need, shall go on, and yet when they return a second time there shall still be plenty; and though they return many times, as long as they live the store shall never fail; and thus they will be supplied with abundance of food without toil." "Not so," said the elder brother, "for then will the people, idle and worthless, and having no labor to perform, engage in quarrels, and fighting will ensue, and they will destroy each other, and the people will be lost to the earth; they must work for all they receive." Then the younger brother answered not, but went away sorrowing.

The next day he met the elder brother and accosted him thus: "Brother, your words were wise; let the *U-ĭn-ká-rĕts* work for their food. But how shall they be furnished with honey-dew? I have thought all night about this, and when the dawn came into the sky I sat on the summit of the mountain and did think, and now I will tell you how to give them honey-dew: Let it fall like a great snow upon the rocks, and the women shall go early in the morning and gather all they may desire, and they shall be glad." "No," replied the elder brother, "it will not be good, my little brother, for them to have much and find it without toil; for they will deem it of no more value than dung, and what we give them for their pleasure will only be wasted. In the night it shall fall in small drops on the reeds, which they shall gather and beat with clubs, and then will it taste very sweet, and having but little they will prize it the more." And the younger brother went away sorrowing, but returned the next day and said: "My brother, your words are wise; let the women gather the honey-dew with much toil, by beating the reeds with flails. Brother, when a man or a woman, or a boy or a girl, or a little one [Pg 45]dies, where shall he go? I have thought all night about this, and when the dawn came into the sky I sat on the top of the mountain and did think. Let me tell you what to do: When a man dies, send him back when the morning returns, and then will all his friends rejoice." "Not so," said the elder; "the dead shall return no more." The little brother answered him not, but, bending his head in sorrow, went away.

One day the younger *Cĭn-aú-äv* was walking in the forest, and saw his brother's son at play, and taking an arrow from his quiver slew the boy, and when he returned he did not mention what he had done. The father supposed that his boy was lost, and wandered around in the woods for many days, and at last found the dead child, and mourned his loss for a long time.

One day the younger *Cĭn-aú-äv* said to the elder, "You made the law that the dead should never return. I am glad that you were the first to suffer." Then the elder knew that the younger had killed his child, and he was very angry and sought to destroy him, and as his wrath increased the earth rocked, subterraneous groanings were heard, darkness came on, fierce storms raged, lightning flashed, thunder reverberated through the heavens, and the younger brother fled in great terror to his father, *Ta-vwots'*, for protection.

ORIGIN OF THE ECHO.

I'-o-wi (the turtle dove) was gathering seeds in the valley, and her little babe slept. Wearied with carrying it on her back, she laid it under the *tĭ-hó-pĭ* (sage bush) in care of its sister,*O-hó-tcu* (the summer yellow bird). Engaged in her labors, the mother wandered away to a distance, when a *tsó-a-vwĭts* (a witch) came and said to the little girl, "Is that your brother?" and *O-hó-tcu* answered, "This is my sister," for she had heard that witches preferred to steal boys, and did not care for girls. Then the *tsó-a-vwĭts* was angry and chided her, saying that it was very naughty for girls to lie; and she put on a strange and horrid appearance, so that *O-hó-tcu* was stupefied with fright; then the *tsó-a-vwĭts* ran away with the boy, carrying him, to her home on a distant mountain. Then she laid him down on the ground, and, taking hold of his right foot, stretched the baby's leg until it was as long as that of a man, and she did the same to the other leg; then his body was elongated; she stretched his arms, and, behold, the baby was as large as a man. And the *tsó-a-vwĭts* married him and had a husband, which she had long desired; but, though he had the body of a man, he had the heart of a babe, and knew no better than to marry a witch.

Now, when *I'-o-wi* returned and found not her babe under the *tĭ-hó-pĭ*, but learned from *O-hó-tcu* that it had been stolen by a *tsó-a-vwĭts*, she was very angry, and punished her daughter very severely. Then she went in search of the babe for a long time, mourning [Pg 46]as she went, and crying and still crying, refusing to be comforted, though all her friends joined her in the search, and promised to revenge her wrongs.

Chief among her friends was her brother, *Kwi'-na*, (the eagle), who traveled far and wide over all the land, until one day he heard a strange noise, and coming near he saw the *tsó-a-vwĭts* and *U'-ja* (the sage cock), her husband, but he did not know that this large man was indeed the little boy who had been stolen. Yet he returned and related to *I'-o-wi* what he had seen, who said: "If that is indeed my boy, he will know my voice." So the mother came near to where the *tsó-a-vwĭts* and *U'-ja* were living, and climbed into a cedar tree, and mourned and cried continually. *Kwi'-na* placed himself near by on another tree to observe what effect the voice of the mother would have on *U'-ja*, the *tsó-a-vwĭts'* husband. When he heard the cry of his mother, *U'-ja* knew the voice, and said to the *tsó-a-vwĭts*, "I hear my mother, I hear my mother, I hear my mother," but she laughed at him, and persuaded him to hide.

Now, the *tsó-a-vwĭts* had taught *U'-ja* to hunt, and a short time before he had killed a mountain sheep, which was lying in camp. The witch emptied the contents of the stomach, and with her husband took refuge within; for she said to herself, "Surely, *I'-o-wi* will never look in the paunch of a mountain sheep for my husband." In this retreat they were safe for a long time, so that they who were searching were sorely puzzled at the strange disappearance. At last *Kwi'-na* said, "They are hid somewhere in the ground, maybe, or under the rocks; after a long time they will be very hungry and will search for food; I will put some in a tree so as to tempt them." So he killed a rabbit and put it on the top of a tall pine, from which he trimmed the branches and peeled the bark, so that it would be very difficult to climb; and he said, "When these hungry people come out they will try to climb that tree for food, and it will take much time, and while the *tsó-a-vwĭts* is thus engaged we will carry *U'-ja* away." So they watched some days, until the *tsó-a-vwĭts* was very hungry, and her baby-hearted husband cried for food; and she came out from their hiding place and sought for something to eat. The odor of the meat placed on the tree came to her nostrils, and she saw where it was and tried to climb up, but fell back many times; and while so doing *Kwi'-na*, who had been sitting on a rock near by and had seen from where she came, ran to the paunch which had been their house, and taking the man carried him away and laid him down under the very same *tĭ-hó-pĭ* from which he had been stolen; and behold! he was the same beautiful little babe that *I'-o-wi* had lost.

And *Kwi'-na* went off into the sky and brought back a storm, and caused the wind to blow, and the rain to beat upon the ground, so that his tracks were covered, and the *tsó-a-vwĭts* could not follow him; but she saw lying upon the ground near by some eagle feathers, and knew well who it was that had deprived her of her husband, and she said to [Pg 47]herself, "Well, I know *Kwi'-na* is the brother of *I'-o-wi*; he is a great warrior and a terrible man; I will go to *To-go'-a* (the rattlesnake), my grandfather, who will protect me and kill my enemies."

To-go'-a was enjoying his midday sleep on a rock, and as the *tsó-a-vwĭts* came near her grandfather awoke and called out to her, "Go back, go back; you are not wanted here; go back!" But she came on begging his protection; and while they were still parleying they heard *Kwi'-na* coming, and *To-go'-a* said, "Hide, hide!" But she knew not where to hide, and he opened his mouth and the *tsó-a-vwĭts* crawled into his stomach. This made *To-go'-a* very sick and he entreated her to crawl out, but she refused, for she was in great fear. Then he tried to throw her up, but could not, and he was sick nigh unto death. At last, in his terrible retchings, he crawled out of his own skin, and left the *tsó-a-vwĭts* in it, and she, imprisoned there, rolled about and hid in the rocks. When *Kwi'-na* came near he shouted, "Where are you, old *tsó-a-vwĭts*? where are you, old *tsó-a-vwĭts*?" She repeated his words in mockery.

Ever since that day witches have lived in snake skins, and hide among the rocks, and take great delight in repeating the words of passers by.

The white man, who has lost the history of these ancient people, calls these mocking cries of witches domiciliated in snake skins "echoes," but the Indians know the voices of the old hags.

This is the origin of the echo.

THE SÓ-KS WAÍ-N-ÄTS.

Tûm-pwĭ-nai'-ro-gwĭ-nûmp, he who had a stone shirt, killed *Sĭ-kor'*, (the crane,) and stole his wife, and seeing that she had a child, and thinking it would be an incumbrance to them on their travels, he ordered her to kill it. But the mother, loving the babe, hid it under her dress, and carried it away to its grandmother. And Stone Shirt carried his captured bride to his own land.

In a few years the child grew to be a fine lad, under the care of his grandmother, and was her companion wherever she went.

One day they were digging flag roots, on the margin of the river, and putting them in a heap on the bank. When they had been at work a little while, the boy perceived that the roots came up with greater ease than was customary, and he asked the old woman the cause of this, but she did not know; and, as they continued their work, still the reeds came up with less effort, at which their wonder increased, until the grandmother said, "Surely, some strange thing is about to transpire." Then the boy went to the heap where they had been placing the roots, and found that some one had taken them away, and he ran back, exclaiming, "Grandmother, did you take the roots away?" And she answered, "No, my child; perhaps [Pg 48]some ghost has taken them off; let us dig no more; come away."

But the boy was not satisfied, as he greatly desired to know what all this meant; so he searched about for a time, and at length found a man sitting under a tree, whom he taunted with being a thief, and threw mud and stones at him, until he broke the stranger's leg, who answered not the boy, nor resented the injuries he received, but remained silent and sorrowful and, when his leg was broken, he tied it up in sticks, and bathed it in the river, and sat down again under the tree, and beckoned the boy to approach.

When the lad came near, the stranger told him he had something of great importance to reveal. "My son," said he, "did that old woman ever tell you about your father and mother?" "No," answered the boy; "I have never heard of them." "My son, do you see these bones scattered on the ground? Whose bones are these?" "How should I know?" answered the boy. "It may be that some elk or deer has been killed here." "No," said the old man. "Perhaps they are the bones of a bear;" but the old man shook his head. So the boy mentioned many other animals, but the stranger still shook his head, and finally said, "These are the bones of your father; Stone Shirt killed him, and left him to rot here on the ground, like a wolf." And the boy was filled with indignation against the slayer of his father. Then the stranger asked, "Is your mother in yonder lodge?" and the boy replied, "No." "Does your mother live on the banks of this river?" and the boy answered, "I don't know my mother; I have never seen her; she is dead." "My son," replied the stranger, "Stone Shirt, who killed your father, stole your mother, and took her away to the shore of a distant lake, and there she is his wife to-day." And the boy wept bitterly, and while the tears filled his eyes so that he could not see, the stranger disappeared.

Then the boy was filled with wonder at what he had seen and heard, and malice grew in his heart against his father's enemy. He returned to the old woman, and said, "Grandmother, why have you lied to me about my father and mother?" and she answered not, for she knew that a ghost had told all to the boy. And the boy fell upon the ground weeping and sobbing, until he fell into a deep sleep, when strange things were told him.

His slumber continued three days and three nights, and when he awoke he said to his grandmother, "I am going away to enlist all nations in my fight," and straightway he departed.

(Here the boy's travels are related with many circumstances concerning the way he was received by the people, all given in a series of conversations, very lengthy; so they will be omitted.)

Finally, he returned in advance of the people whom he had enlisted, bringing with him *Cĭn-au'-äv*, the wolf, and *To-go'-a*, the rattlesnake. When the three had eaten food, the boy said to the old woman: "Grandmother, cut me in two." But she demurred, saying she did not wish to kill one whom she loved so dearly. "Cut me in two," demanded [Pg 49]the boy, and he gave her a stone ax which he had brought from a distant country, and with a manner of great authority he again commanded her to cut him in two. So she stood before him, and severed him in twain, and fled in terror. And lo! each part took the form of an entire man, and the one beautiful boy appeared as two, and they were so much alike no one could tell them apart.

When the people or natives whom the boy had enlisted came pouring into the camp, *Cĭn-au'-äv* and *To-go'-a* were engaged in telling them of the wonderful thing that had happened to the boy, and that now there were two; and they all held it to be an augury of a successful expedition to the land of Stone Shirt. And they started on their journey.

Now the boy had been told in the dream of his three days' slumber of a magical cup, and he had brought it home with him from his journey among the nations, and the *So'-kûs Wai'-ûn-äts* carried it between them, filled with water. *Cĭn-au'-äv* walked on their right and *To-go'-a* on their left, and the nations followed in the order in which they had been enlisted. There was a vast number of them, so that when they were stretched out in line it was one day's journey from the front to the rear of the column.

When they had journeyed two days and were far out on the desert all the people thirsted, for they found no water, and they fell down upon the sand groaning, and murmuring that they had been deceived, and they cursed the One-Two.

But the *So'-kûs Wai'-ûn-äts* had been told in the wonderful dream of the suffering which would be endured and that the water which they carried in the cup was only to be used in dire necessity, and the brothers said to each other: "Now the time has come for us to drink the water." And when one had quaffed of the magical bowl, he found it still full, and he gave it to the other to drink, and still it was full; and the One-Two gave it to the people, and one after another did they all drink, and still the cap was full to the brim.

But *Cĭn-au'-äv* was dead, and all the people mourned, for he was a great man. The brothers held the cup over him, and sprinkled him with water, when he arose and said: "Why do you disturb me? I did have a vision of mountain brooks and meadows, of cane where honey-dew was plenty." They gave him the cup, and he drank also; but when he had finished there was none left. Refreshed and rejoicing they proceeded on their journey.

The next day, being without food, they were hungry, and all were about to perish; and again they murmured at the brothers, and cursed them. But the *So'-kûs Wai'-ûn-*

äts saw in the distance an antelope, standing on an eminence in the plain, in bold relief against the sky; and *Cĭn-au'-äv* knew it was the wonderful antelope with many eyes, which Stone Shirt kept for his watchman; and he proposed to go and kill it, but *To-go'-a* demurred, and said: "It were better that I should go, for he will see you and run away." But the *So'-kûs Wai'-ûn-äts* told Cĭn'-au'-äv to go; and he started in a direction away to the left [Pg 50]of where the antelope was standing, that he might make a long detour about some hills, and come upon him from the other side. *To-go'-a* went a little way from camp, and called to the brothers: "Do you see me?" and they answered they did not. "Hunt for me;" and while they were hunting for him, the rattlesnake said: "I can see you; you are doing"—so and so, telling them what they were doing; but they could not find him.

Then, the rattlesnake came forth, declaring: "Now you know I can see others, and that I cannot be seen when I so desire. *Cin-au'-äv* cannot kill that antelope, for he has many eyes, and is the wonderful watchman of Stone Shirt; but I can kill him, for I can go where he is and he cannot see me." So the brothers were convinced, and permitted him to go; and he went and killed the antelope. When *Cin-au'-äv* saw it fall, he was very angry, for he was extremely proud of his fame as a hunter, and anxious to have the honor of killing this famous antelope, and he ran up with the intention of killing *To-go'-a*; but when he drew near, and saw the antelope was fat, and would make a rich feast for the people, his anger was appeased. "What matters it," said he, "who kills the game, when we can all eat it?"

So all the people were fed in abundance, and they proceeded on their journey.

The next day the people again suffered for water, and the magical cup was empty; but the *So'-kûs Wai'-ûn-äts*, having been told in their dream what to do, transformed themselves into doves, and flew away to a lake, on the margin of which was the home of Stone Shirt.

Coming near to the shore, they saw two maidens bathing in the water; and the birds stood and looked, for the maidens were very beautiful. Then they flew into some bushes, near by, to have a nearer view, and were caught in a snare which the girls had placed for intrusive birds. The beautiful maidens came up, and, taking the birds out of the snare, admired them very much, for they had never seen such birds before. They carried them to their father, Stone Shirt, who said: "My daughters, I very much fear these are spies from my enemies, for such birds do not live in our land"; and he was about to throw them into the fire, when the maidens besought him, with tears, that he would not destroy their beautiful birds; but he yielded to their entreaties with much misgiving. Then they took the birds to the shore of the lake, and set them free.

When the birds were at liberty once more, they flew around among the bushes, until they found the magical cup which they had lost, and taking it up, they carried it out into the middle of the lake and settled down upon the water, and the maidens supposed they were drowned.

The birds, when they had filled their cup, rose again, and went back to the people in the desert, where they arrived just at the right time to save them with the cup of water, from which each drank; and yet it was [Pg 51]full until the last was satisfied, and then not a drop remained.

The brothers reported that they had seen Stone Shirt and his daughters.

The next day they came near to the home of the enemy, and the brothers, in proper person, went out to reconnoiter. Seeing a woman gleaning seeds, they drew near, and knew it was their mother, whom Stone Shirt had stolen from *Sĭ-kor'*, the crane. They told her they were her sons, but she denied it, and said she had never had but one son; but the boys related to her their history, with the origin of the two from one, and she was convinced. She tried to dissuade them from making war upon Stone Shirt, and told them that no arrow could possibly penetrate his armor, and that he was a great warrior, and had no other delight than in killing his enemies, and that his daughters also were furnished with magical bows and arrows, which they could shoot so fast that the arrows would fill the air like a cloud, and that it was not necessary for them to take aim, for their missiles went where they willed; they *thought* the arrows to the hearts of their enemies; and thus the maidens could kill the whole of the people before a common arrow could be shot by a common person. But the boys told her what the spirit had said in the long dream, and had promised that Stone Shirt should be killed. They told her to go down to the lake at dawn, so as not to be endangered by the battle.

During the night, the *So'-kûs Wai'-ûn-äts* transformed themselves into mice, and proceeded to the home of Stone Shirt, and found the magical bows and arrows that belonged to the maidens, and with their sharp teeth they cut the sinew on the backs of the bows, and nibbled the bowstrings, so that they were worthless, while *To-go'-a* hid himself under a rock near by.

When dawn came into the sky, *Tûm-pwĭ-nai'-ro-gwĭ-nûmp*, the Stone Shirt man, arose and walked out of his tent, exulting in his strength and security, and sat down upon the rock under which *To-go'-a* was hiding; and he, seeing his opportunity, sunk his fangs into the flesh of the hero. Stone Shirt sprang high into the air, and called to his daughters that they were betrayed, and that the enemy was near; and they seized their magical bows, and their quivers filled with magical arrows, and hurried to his defense. At the same time, all the nations who were surrounding the camp rushed down to battle. But the beautiful maidens, finding their weapons were destroyed, waved back their enemies, as if they would parley; and, standing for a few moments over the body of their slain father, sang the death-song, and danced the death-dance, whirling in giddy circles about the dead hero, and wailing with despair, until they sank down and expired.

The conquerers buried the maidens by the shores of the lake; but *Tûm-pwĭ-nai'-ro-gwĭ-nûmp* was left to rot, and his bones to [Pg 52]bleach on the sands, as he had left *Sĭ-kor'*.

TA-VWOTS' HAS A FIGHT WITH THE SUN.

Ta-vwots', the little rabbit, was wont to lie with his back to the sun when he slept. One day he thus slept in camp while his children played around him. After a time they saw that his back was smoking, and they cried out "What is the matter with your back, father?" Startled from his sleep, he demanded to know the cause of the uproar. "Your back is covered with sores and full of holes," they replied. Then *Ta-vwots'* was very angry, for he knew that *Ta'-vĭ*, the sun, had burned him; and he sat down by the fire for a long time in solemn mood, pondering on the injury and insult he had received. At last rising to his feet, he said, "My children I must go and make war upon *Ta'-vĭ*." And straightway he departed.

Now his camp was in the valley of the Mo-a-pa. [1] On his journey he came to a hill, and standing on its summit he saw in a valley to the east a beautiful stretch of verdure, and he greatly marveled at the sight and desired to know what it was. On going down to the valley he found a corn-field, something he had never before seen, and the ears were ready for roasting. When he examined them, he saw that they were covered with beautiful hair, and he was much astonished. Then he opened the husk and found within soft white grains of corn, which he tasted. Then he knew that it was corn and good to eat. Plucking his arms full he carried them away, roasted them on a fire, and ate until he was filled.

Now, when he had done all this, he reflected that he had been stealing, and he was afraid; so he dug a hole in which to hide himself.

Cĭn-au'-äv was the owner of this field, and when he walked through and saw that his corn had been stolen, he was exceedingly wroth, and said, "I will slay this thief *Ta-vwots'*; I will kill him, I will kill him." And straightway he called his warriors to him and made search for the thief, but could not find him, for he was hid in the ground. After a long time they discovered the hole and tried to shoot *Ta-vwots'* as he was standing in the entrance, but he blew their arrows back. This made *Cĭn-au'-äv's* people very angry and they shot many arrows, but *Ta-vwots"* breath as a warder, against them all. Then, with one accord, they ran to snatch him up with their hands, but, all in confusion, they only caught each others fists, for with agile steps *Ta-vwots'* dodged into his retreat. Then they began to dig, and said they would drag him out. And they labored with great energy, all the time taunting him with shouts and jeers. But *Ta-*

vwots' had a secret passage from the main chamber of his retreat which opened by a hole above the rock overhanging the entrance where they were at work.

[Pg 53]

When they had proceeded with this digging until they were quite under ground, *Ta-vwots'*, standing on the rock above, hurled the magical ball which he was accustomed to carry with him, and striking the ground above the diggers, it caved the earth in, and they were all buried. "Aha," said he, "why do you wish to hinder me on my way to kill the Sun? *A'-nier ti-tĭk'-a-nûmp kwaik-ai'-gar*" (fighting is my eating tool I say; that's so!), and he proceeded on his way musing. "I have started out to kill; vengeance is my work; every one I meet will be an enemy. It is well; no one shall escape my wrath."

The next day he saw two men making arrow-heads of hot rocks, and drawing near he observed their work for a time from a position where he could not be seen. Then stepping forth, he said: "Let me help you"; and when the rocks were on the fire again and were hot to redness he said: "Hot rocks will not burn me." And they laughed at him. "May be you would have us believe that you are a ghost?" "I am not a ghost," said he, "but I am a better man than you are. Hold me on these hot rocks, and if I do not burn you must let me do the same to you." To this they readily agreed, and when they had tried to burn him on the rocks, with his magic breath he kept them away at a distance so slight they could not see but that the rocks did really touch him. When they perceived that he was not burned they were greatly amazed and trembled with fear. But having made the promise that he should treat them in like manner, they submitted themselves to the torture, and the hot rocks burned them until with great cries they struggled to get free but unrelenting *Ta-vwots'* held them until the rocks had burned through their flesh into their entrails, and so they died. "Aha," said *Ta-vwots'*, "lie there until you can get up again. I am on my way to kill the Sun. *A'-nier ti-tĭk'-a-nûmp kwaik-ai'-gar.*" And sounding the war-whoop he proceeded on his way.

The next day he came to where two women were gathering berries in baskets, and when he sat down they brought him some of the fruit and placed it before him. He saw there were many leaves and thorns among the berries, and he said, "Blow these leaves and thorns into my eyes," and they did so, hoping to blind him; but with his magic breath he kept them away, so that they did not hurt him.

Then the women averred that he was a ghost. "I am no ghost," said he, "but a common person; do you not know that leaves and thorns cannot hurt the eye? Let me show you;" and they consented and were made blind. Then *Ta-vwots'* slew them with his *pa-rûm'-o-kwi*. "Aha," said he, "you are caught with your own chaff. I am on my way to kill the Sun. This is good practice. I must learn how. *A'-nier ti-tĭk'-a-nûmp kwaik-ai'-gar.*" And sounding the war-whoop he proceeded on his way.

The next day he saw some women standing on the Hurricane Cliff, and as he approached he heard them say to each other that they would roll rocks [Pg 54]down upon his head and kill him as he passed; and drawing near he pretended to be eating something, and enjoying it with great gusto; so they asked him what it was, and he said it was something very sweet, and they begged that they might be allowed to taste of it also. "I will throw it up to you," said he; "come to the brink and catch it." When they had done so, he threw it up so that they could not quite reach it, and he threw it in this way many times, until, in their eagerness to secure it, they all crowded too near the brink, fell, and were killed. "Aha," said he, "you were killed by your own eagerness. I am on my way to kill the Sun. *A'-nier ti-tĭk'-a-nûmp kaiwk-ai'-gar.*" And sounding the war-whoop he passed on.

The following day he saw two women fashioning water-jugs, which are made of willow-ware like baskets and afterwards lined with pitch. When afar off he could hear them converse, for he had a wonderful ear. "Here comes that bad *Ta-vwots'*," said they; "how shall we destroy him?" When he came near, he said, "What was that you were saying when I came up?" "Oh, we were only saying, 'here comes our grandson,'"[2] said they. "Is that all?" replied *Ta-vwots'*, and looking around, he said, "Let me get into your water-jug"; and they allowed him to do so. "Now braid the neck." This they did, making the neck very small; then they laughed with great glee, for they supposed he was entrapped. But with his magic breath he burst the jug, and stood up before them; and they exclaimed, "You must be a ghost!" but he answered, "I am no ghost. Do you not know that jugs were made to hold water, but cannot hold men and women?" At this they wondered greatly, and said he was wise. Then he proposed to put them in jugs in the same manner, in order to demonstrate to them the truth of what he had said; and they consented. When he had made the necks of the jugs and filled them with pitch, he said, "Now, jump out," but they could not. It was now his turn to deride; so he rolled them about and laughed greatly, while their half-stifled screams rent the air. When he had sported with them in this way until he was tired, he killed them with his magical ball. "Aha," said he, "you are bottled in your own jugs. I am on my way to kill the Sun; in good time I shall learn how. *A'-nier ti-tĭk'-a-nûmp kaiwk-ai'-gar.*" And sounding the war-whoop he passed on.

The next day he came upon *Kwi'-ats*, the bear, who was digging a hole in which to hide, for he had heard of the fame of *Ta-vwots'*, and was afraid. When the great slayer came to *Kwi'-ats* he said, "Don't fear, my great friend; I am not the man from whom to hide. Could a little fellow like me kill so many people?" And the bear was assured. "Let me help you dig," said *Ta-vwots'*, that we may hide together, for I also am fleeing from the great destroyer. So they made a den deep in the ground, with its entrance concealed by a great rock. Now, *Ta-vwots'* secretly made a private passage from the den out to the side of the mountain, and when the work was completed the two went out together to [Pg 55]the hill-top to watch for the coming of the enemy.

Soon *Ta-vwots'* pretended that he saw him coming, and they ran in great haste to the den. The little one outran the greater, and going into the den, hastened out again through his secret passage.

When *Kwi'-ats* entered he looked about, and not seeing his little friend he searched for him for some time, and still not finding him, he supposed that he must have passed him on the way, and went out again to see if he had stopped or been killed. By this time *Ta-vwots'* had perched himself on the rock at the entrance of the den, and when the head of the bear protruded through the hole below he hurled his *pa-rûm'-o-kwi* and killed him. "Aha," said *Ta-vwots'*, "I greatly feared this renowned warrior, but now he is dead in his own den. I am going to kill the Sun. *A'-nier ti'-tĭk'-a'-nûmp kwaik-ai'-gar.*" And sounding the war-whoop he went on his way.

The next day he met *Ku-mi'-a-pöts*, the tarantula. Now this knowing personage had heard of the fame of *Ta-vwots'*, and determined to outwit him. He was possessed of a club with such properties that, although it was a deadly weapon when used against others, it could not be made to hurt himself, though wielded by a powerful arm.

As *Ta-vwots'* came near, *Ku-mi'-a-pöts* complained of having a headache; moaning and groaning, he said there was an *u-nu'-pĭts*, or little evil spirit, in his head, and he asked *Ta-vwots'* to take the club and beat it out. *Ta-vwots'* obeyed, and struck with all his power, and wondered that *Ku-mi'-a-pöts* was not killed; but he urged *Ta-vwots'* to strike harder. At last *Ta-vwots'* understood the nature of the club, and guessed the wiles of *Ku-mi'-a-pöts*, and raising the weapon as if to strike again, he dexterously substituted his magic ball and slew him. "Aha," said he, "that is a blow of your own seeking, *Ku-mi'-a-pöts*. I am on my way to kill the Sun; now I know that I can do it. *A'-nier ti'-tĭk'-a'-nûmp kwaik-ai'-gar.*" And sounding the war-whoop he went on his way.

The next day he came to a cliff which is the edge or boundary of the world on the east, where careless persons have fallen into unknown depths below. Now to come to the summit of this cliff it is necessary to climb a mountain, and *Ta-vwots'* could see three gaps or notches in the mountain, and he went up into the one on the left; and he demanded to know of all the trees which where standing by of what use they were. Each one in turn praised its own qualities, the chief of which in every case was its value as fuel.[3] *Ta-vwots'* shook his head and went into the center gap and had another conversation with the trees, receiving the same answer. Finally he went into the third gap—that on the right. After he had questioned all the trees and bushes, he came at last to a little one called *yu'-i-nump*, which modestly said it had no use, that it was not even fit for fuel. "Good," said *Ta-vwots'*, and under it he lay down to sleep.

When the dawn came into the sky *Ta-vwots'* arose and stood on the brink overhanging the abyss from which the Sun was about to rise. The instant it appeared he hurled

www.ingramcontent.com/pod-product-compliance
Lightning Source LLC
Chambersburg PA
CBHW080024130526
44591CB00036B/2638

his *pa-rûm'-o-kwi*, and, striking it full in the face, shattered it into innumerable fragments, and these fragments were scattered over all the world and kindled a great conflagration. *Ta-vwots'* ran and crept under the *yu'-i-nump* to obtain protection. At last the fire waxed very hot over all the world, and soon *Ta-vwots* began to suffer and tried to ran away, but as he ran his toes were burned off, and then slowly, inch by inch, his legs, and then his body, so that he walked on his hands, and these were burned, and he walked on the stumps of his arms, and these were burned, until there was nothing left but his head. And now, having no other means of progression, his head rolled along the ground until his eyes, which were much swollen, burst by striking against a rock, and the tears gushed out in a great flood which spread out over all the land and extinguished the conflagration.

The *Uinta Utes* add something more to this story, namely, that the flood from his eyes bore out new seeds, which were scattered over all the world. The *Ute* name for seed is the same as for eye.

Those animals which are considered as the descendants of *Ta-vwots'* are characterized by a brown patch back of the neck and shoulders, which is attributed to the singeing received by him in the great fire.

The following apothegms are derived from this story:

"You are buried in the hole which you dug for yourself."

"When you go to war every one you meet is an enemy; kill all."

"You were caught with your own chaff."

"Don't get so anxious that you kill yourself."

"You are bottled in your own jugs."

"He is dead in his own den."

"That is a blow of your own seeking."
